THE GREAT AMERICAN DIVIDE: THE MILITARY-CIVILIAN GAP

"We the people of the United States, in order to form a more perfect union, establish justice, insure domestic tranquility, provide for the common defense ... do ordain and establish this Constitution for the United States of America."[1] Such are the words to the Preamble to the Constitution that is the basis for how the American people govern themselves. Of particular note are the phrases "we the people" and "provide for the common defense" that enshrine the idea of shared sacrifice among all the American people in protecting and defending the United States. For much of the United States' history, this idea of shared sacrifice in the defense of the nation has been exercised and heartily supported by every race, religion, sex, and socio-economic class of the American people. However, in the years since the advent of the all volunteer military, the American people have increasingly distanced themselves from the idea of shared sacrifice and have grown complacent with having a small, narrow segment of the American population carry the burden of providing for the common defense through military service. This trend, the military – civilian gap, is creating a separate and distinct military class of society that is in danger of becoming disconnected from the greater American society they are sworn to protect. The military – civilian gap is at risk of producing a military that increasingly sees itself as superior to society and is susceptible to a group think mentality. Conversely, the military – civilian gap is producing a civilian population governed by civilian leaders that have an inadequate understanding of military force, its limitations, and its true costs in lives and treasure in providing for the security of the nation. Taken to its extreme, the military – civilian gap can result in a military that is contemptuous of the greater American society and an American public that is so disconnected from the military class that it fails to value or question the employment of American military forces.

To a certain degree, a military-civilian gap is almost inevitable. Historically when looking at the total number of military service members compared to that of the total United States population, the military has always been a small percentage of that total population. Even at the conclusion of World War II, when over 16 million Americans had served in the armed forces, only 11.4% of the United States population had served in the United States military.[2] Today, the large disparity between those serving/having served in the military and the rest of the non-serving population is caused by many factors. Chief among those factors is government economics, or how much military the United States can afford, as this limits the number of people that can serve in the military. Combine government economics with the age limitations and the physical requirements of military service and it is understandable why such a small percentage of the United States population serves in the military. Accepting that military service will always represent a minority of the total United States population, what are the "gap" areas that are most detrimental to the military-civilian relationship? What actions, if any, can be taken to mitigate these detrimental gap areas? In searching for answers to these questions, it may be helpful to first understand the composition/demographics of the United States military.

Demographics

The armed forces of the United States constitute one of the most diverse organizations in the world. Some level of representation of almost every race, ethnic group, and religion can be found in the United States military. The most recent racial/ethnic group data for the United States Armed Forces from 2010 shows that the active duty military is 70% white, 17% black, 13.1% other, with 11.2% of active service members identifying themselves as ethnic Hispanics.[3] By comparison, the racial/ethnic population of the United States in 2010 was 72.4% white, 12.6% black, 15% other, with 16.3% of the United States population identifying themselves as ethnic Hispanics.[4] While the specific levels of race and ethnic group representation in the military can fluctuate in any given year, the 2010 military racial/ethnic group demographics follow the historical norms of demographic trends in the all volunteer force since 1973.[5] In terms of a potential racial/ethnic group military-civilian gap, the military is relatively representative of the United States population as a whole with a slightly higher density of minorities, particularly black Americans, in the military than are found in the United States civilian population.

Is the racial/ethnic group demographic an area of concern towards a military-civilian gap? Not directly, but it is likely that the military's racial/ethnic group demographics and the military's emphasis on equal opportunity is divergent from the greater civilian population. While the military is fairly racially/ethnically representative of civilian society, the military views itself as a much more racially/ethnically integrated and equal society. This view stems from its racial history and the military's focus on team building. Historically, the military was on the leading edge of equality/integration and was the first major institution in the United States to do so through Presidential Executive Order 9981 in 1948.[6] Executive Order 9981 not only forced the integration of military units, but also forced the integration of Department of Defense schools, and military installation neighborhoods and facilities. Over the past 60 years the military has been an integrated society where today the cultural norm is to support equal opportunity in all facets of military life. Equal opportunity oriented considerations are built into each of the military services evaluation reports and promotion board systems to ensure non-discriminatory practices. While great strides in racial equality have been made in civilian society, the military has typically led civilian society in this regard and in many aspects continues to do so today. In their book, *All That We Can Be: Black Leadership and Racial Integration the Army Way*, sociologists Charles Moskos and John Butler describe how the Army's racial equality and integration has led that of civilian society as follows:

> One major American institution, however, contradicts the prevailing race paradigm. It is an organization unmatched in its level of racial integration. It is an institution unmatched in its broad record of black achievement. It is a world in which Afro-American heritage is part and parcel of the institutional culture. It is the only place in American life where whites are routinely bossed around by blacks. The institution is the U.S. Army.[7]

While integration is the accepted cultural norm in military society, civilian society still harbors pockets of segregation whether from socio-economic, education, or other causes. For example, many living spaces and neighborhoods in civilian society remain segregated today in the form of "white only" and "minority only" neighborhoods in many cities and towns throughout the United States. A 2010 study of the 20 most multiethnic metropolitan regions in the United States found that "half the black population and 40 percent of Hispanics still live in neighborhoods without a white presence."[8] Furthermore, the military's focus on "the team" and the team building aspects of the military may also account for why it sees itself as a more integrated and equal society than civilian society. Practically every activity in the military depends on a team that is cohesive, trained, and efficient in executing their duties. Because the importance of being a team is instilled into every military member upon entry into the service, military members tend to see one another as teammates and less so as a person of a specific race or ethnic group. These positive racial aspects of the military may be one of the reasons the black population is represented in higher numbers in the military than in civilian society.

Geography also provides some interesting insights into the composition of the United States' military. For the 37 year period from 1973 to 2010, the South has provided the overwhelming number of service members to the military at 37.5%, followed by the North Central region at 24.6%, the West at 19.5%, the Northeast at 17.3%, and all other areas at 1.2%.[9] Since 1990 the trend in geographic accessions has seen the South increase to 41.7%, the West increase to 21.5%, other areas increase to 1.3%, with decreases in the North Central region to 21.3%, and the Northeast to 14.2%.[10] Based on these numbers, it is evident that the South produces military members at a rate almost twice that of any other region in the United States. To a degree, it is not surprising that the South produces more military recruits than any other region; the Southern region is the most populated region of the United States which would lead the military to have a heavy recruitment focus in the Southern region.[11] The large percentage of recruits from the South may provide another reason the military has a slightly higher representation of blacks than civilian society. The South has a higher preponderance of 18 to 24 year old blacks than other regions of the United States.[12] In 2010, blacks comprised 22.5% of the Southern regions 18 to 24 year old demographic.[13] Correspondingly, black recruits accounted for 24% of the total recruits from the Southern Region.[14] The 2010 data is representative of the historical norm since 1996 in that Southern blacks have typically provided slightly higher numbers of military service members as compared to their overall representation in Southern civilian society.[15] However, the number of black recruits from the South has not been to such a degree that it would produce overwhelmingly higher numbers of blacks in the military than is found in civilian society.

The basing of active duty military forces is also dominated by the Southern region of the United States. Currently, 57.1% of active duty forces are based in the South, 31.7% of forces are based in the West, 7.4% are based in North Central, and 3.6% of active duty forces are based in the Northeast region.[16] This hierarchy of active duty military basing (South, West, North Central, Northeast) matches that of the active duty assessments geographic hierarchy since 1990. This may indicate that active duty military basing does, in some way, affect military recruitment. Military bases provide tremendous conduits for the military to develop relationships and partnerships with the civilian communities in which they are located. In essence, civilians get to know the military through the active duty forces based in their community which breeds familiarity, understanding, and support for the military. With over half the active duty forces located in the Southern United States and a focused Southern region recruitment effort, it is little wonder that the United States military is becoming a Southern dominated institution.

While the South has historically been a strong contributor to the nation's defense, the trend of the Northeast providing fewer and fewer service members highlights a growing divide in the nation's burden sharing for national defense. Particularly troubling about the Northeast's decreasing interest in military service is that Northeast institutions tend to be the wellspring for the nation's social and political elite.

The Ivy League colleges of Brown, Dartmouth, Yale, Harvard, Princeton, Cornell, Columbia, and the University of Pennsylvania have historically produced high percentages of the upper classes commanding both industry and government. For example, seven of the last 13 Presidents have been Ivy League alumni, all current serving Supreme Court justices are Ivy League alumni, and with the exception of 1964, there has been at least one Ivy League alumnus on either the Republican or Democratic national Presidential tickets since 1932.[17] Two of the top three colleges for serving members of Congress are Harvard and Yale.[18] In the corporate world, five of the top 10 institutions that awarded degrees to 125 of the Chief Executive Officers of Fortune 500 companies are Ivy League schools.[19] Yet for all the willingness of the Ivy League elite to serve in the highest positions of civilian society and government, the willingness of their graduates to serve in the military has greatly diminished over the years. Frank Schaeffer, in his book *AWOL, The Unexcused Absence of America's Upper Classes from Military Service* states that "in 1956, 400 out of 750 in Princeton's graduating class went into the military. In contrast, in 2004, nine members of Princeton's graduating class entered the services, and they led the Ivy League in numbers".[20] A recent article on Ivy League Reserve Officers Training Corps by the strategic studies scholar Eliot A. Cohen opines that "students who go to top colleges and universities are smart, hardworking and able. Our armed forces need them...these young people, who will some day run our businesses and our politics, should share the burden of national defense."[21]

While the Ivy League produces a disproportionate number of corporate and civilian government elite compared to their representation in the military, they are by no means alone in lacking of military experience. The elite of the legislative, executive, and judicial branches of government are also areas of concern in regards to military veteran representation. Legislatively, the United States Congress is becoming more and more separated from the military with every election. In the 91st Congress (1969-1971) over 74% of those elected to the Congress were military veterans.[22] In the 96th Congress (1979-1981) the number of Congressional veterans had dropped to 55%[23] and continued to decrease in subsequent elections that by the 107th Congress (2001-2003) the number of Congressional veterans were at 31%.[24] Currently, only 22% of the 112th Congress (2011-2013) has any military service experience and the downward trend of military veterans serving in Congress continues.[25] Political science researchers William T. Bianco and Jamie Markham offer an explanation for the ever declining veteran representation in Congress:

> Absent universal conscription, such as occurred in World War II and Korea, individuals with high educational levels and high socio-economic status, who are disproportionately more likely to serve as congressional candidates, are less likely to serve in the military compared to individuals who are less educated and of a lower socio-economic status. In an era marked by universal conscription, these behavioral differences wash out: essentially everyone becomes a veteran, because no one has a choice. But when military service becomes an option, as it increasingly did in the 1960's and thereafter, it would be no surprise to find that the kinds of people who typically serve in Congress are likely to remain civilians....While the probability of military service has been falling for everyone over the last two generations, it has been falling at a greater rate for the people who typically run for Congress compared to the rest of the population. As a result, there are fewer and fewer veterans in younger congressional cohorts. Moreover, in the absence of some form of universal conscription, this asymmetry is unlikely to change.[26]

Presidential military experience has historically been well represented as 32 of the 44 Presidents of the United States have had military experience. However, as is the case with Congress, presidential military experience has also seen declines since 1993 with two of the last three Presidents having had no military experience. Based on current political trends, the 2012 presidential election will also likely result in a president without military experience since President Obama and the likely Republican candidate, Mitt Romney, Rick Santorum, or Newt Gingrich, have never served in the military.[27] Because more and more aspiring presidential candidates do not have military experience, it is quite possible that "veteran status has become a less politically valuable characteristic for a would-be candidate."[28]

<u>Gaps and Causes</u>

Perhaps the widest gulf between civilians and the military resides in the military culture/society. Attitudes and views prevalent within the military are frequently at odds with or not shared by the general civilian society. It does not take long for a new military recruit to realize that military society is considerably different than civilian society. At the earliest stages of military training, drill instructors often chide fresh recruits to leave their civilian habits behind while introducing them to a more disciplined and team-oriented society. Recruits learn to accept the rank-structured system with its own military lingo, which, for example, even tells time in a way different from civilian society. By the time a recruit completes his or her initial entry training and becomes a full fledged Soldier, Sailor, Marine, or Airmen, that person has accepted a whole new lifestyle and is ready to become a contributing member to the military society. What is interesting about the military society is that no one is born into this society.[29] People from every race, religion, ethnic group, education level, and socio-economic background are represented in the military society but they must all earn their way into this society through the military initial entry training process. Because the military is ultimately responsible for fighting and winning the nation's wars, discipline is the cornerstone of the military society. In addition to discipline, military leaders have found it necessary to recognize a value system that guides behavior in the military society. As a result, each of the services has reduced to writing a set of core values that it expects its members to live by. While each service has espoused a slightly different set of core values, all share common themes that form the values of military society. Some would argue that military leaders were compelled to instill military society values in its recruits due to civilian society's failure to provide American youth with militarily compatible values or any values at all.[30]

The result of adopting a set of core military values is that military society views itself as living by a higher moral code than is generally practiced in the larger civilian society. In a 1997 radio interview, military sociologist Charles Moskos stated "there is a kind of a widespread mood throughout the armed forces that ... civilian society's getting softer, more corrupt, less moral and that the military stands out ... different and apart, in harking to a higher standard."[31] In fact this characteristic has been something of a selling point in military recruiting. The idea of joining a technologically advanced, elite warrior caste is a common theme in recruiting materials.[32] Military recruiting, particularly the Marines, evoke the notion that individuals are joining a better, more professional group than is found in civilian society and statistically, the military recruiting slogans are correct.[33] Out of the target market for military recruitment, only 25% of the youth between the ages of 18 and 24 qualify for military service due to physical issues, moral issues (e.g., criminal record, drug dependency etc.), or failure to have a high school diploma.[34] Compared to civilian society the military is better educated with over 99.5%

of the military having a high school diploma and 79% of the active military having some additional education less than a Bachelors Degree.[35] Whereas civilian society has 86.3% high school graduates and only 27% with additional education less than a Bachelors Degree.[36] Furthermore, since 1983 the military has assessed more people with higher aptitudes as measured by the Armed Forces Qualification Tests than are found in the civilian population.[37] In 2010, 68.9% of the assessed military recruits scored better (50th percentile or higher) than the national average on the Armed Forces Qualification Tests.[38] Eliot A. Cohen states "that the military has come to see itself as an organization with better values and more functional social behavior than civil society" and "marks yet another departure from the past, when the armed forces saw themselves more as a reflection of society and less as its superior."[39]

Views and opinions are also a defining characteristic of the military-civilian gap. In a recent Pew Research Center study, several interesting differences between post-9/11 veteran and civilian attitudes and opinions were discovered.[40] Politically, the post-9/11 veterans described themselves as 36% Republican, 21% Democrat, and 35% Independent.[41] Almost the opposite, the civilian public described themselves as 23% Republican, 34% Democrat, and 35% Independent.[42] In a more focused study, Heidi A. Urben, in her doctoral dissertation *Civil-Military Relations in a Time of War: Party, Politics, and the Profession of Arms*, conducted a survey of approximately 4000 Army Officers ranging from Lieutenant to Colonel and recorded their political and ideological attitudes. Out of the 3,907 Army Officers that provided responses, 60% identified themselves as Republican, 18% as Democrat, and 15% as Independent.[43] Both the Pew Research and Heidi Urben's survey results are also relatively consistent with political affiliation trends as found in the 1998-1999 Triangle Institute for Security Studies (TISS) Survey on the Military in the Post-Cold War Era.[44] Taken as a whole, these three surveys indicate a consistency over time of military/veterans being more Republican than Democrat in terms of political party affiliation than their civilian counterparts particularly in the officer ranks.

The Pew survey also found a significant gap between post-9/11 veterans and civilians on whether they would advise a young person to join the military. 82% of post-9/11 veterans surveyed said they would recommend military service to young adults as compared to only 48% of the general public.[45] This tremendous difference of opinion indicates that military veterans value their military experience at a much higher rate than civilian society. This result may also be reflective of the civilian population having little understanding of the military and thus being hesitant to provide advice to young people on a career or job in which they have no experience. When asked questions on their understanding of the military, 54% of the public responded that they did not understand the benefits and rewards of military service, with 71% of the public responding that they do not understand the problems those in the military face.[46] Correspondingly, 73% of post-9/11 veterans do not think the public understands the benefits and rewards of military service followed by 84% of post-9/11 veterans believing the public does not understand the problems faced by those in the military.[47]

Perhaps the most significant information contained in the Pew Research Center study are the findings surrounding the idea of shared sacrifice and how the American public is disconnected from the current war on terror. The Pew study found that 50% of the American public feels that the wars in Afghanistan and Iraq have made little difference in their lives and only 36% say that the war ever comes up in conversation with family or friends.[48] When the public is asked a series of questions about making sacrifices since the 9/11 attacks, 83% of the American public thinks the military and their families have made a lot of sacrifices while 43% believe the American public have made a lot of sacrifices.[49] While these findings show that the American public clearly believes the military has made a lot of sacrifices since 9/11, surprisingly, Pew found that in a comparative analysis, only 47% of the American public rates the military's sacrifice as greater than that of the public's. Even more surprising is that out of those 47% in the American public who rate the military as having sacrificed more since 9/11, an overwhelming majority, 70% of the public respondents, see nothing unfair with the military sacrificing more than other citizens as they believe it is just part of being in the military.[50] If the Pew Research Center's findings on shared sacrifice are truly indicative of the American society, then the military-civilian gap may be at a wider gulf than many suspected.

Concerns and Consequences

While there are many facets to the divergences between the military and civilian society, there are three divergent trends that are increasing at a higher rate than at any time since World War II. These divergent trends are the military's internal views of the superiority of its values and culture, civilian society's inadequate experience with and understanding of the military, and the unequal burden in shared sacrifice. Each of these divergent trends has the potential to negatively affect civil-military relations and is ultimately detrimental to national security.

The military's view of its values and culture being superior to civilian society are driven from its self-perceptions of being a more educated and disciplined society with higher moral values and a stronger work ethic. These perceptions combined with a particular ideology can be an explosive combination that may invite a group think mentality that can limit possibilities and options. In some cases it can border on arrogance and lead to an attitude that the military, not the civilian leadership, have a better understanding of a situation and official policy should reflect the military's view. A recent example of this issue can be found in the book *Obama's Wars*, by Bob Woodward.

In *Obama's Wars* Woodward provides an account of the contentious discussions between the Obama administration and military leaders concerning General Stanley McChrystal's August 2009 Afghanistan assessment and the policy recommendations for the President.[51] After several months of internal debate and requests for new strategies, President Obama lamented that "he just kept getting the same old options" from Admiral Michael Mullen, General David Petraeus, and General McChrystal. All three repeatedly recommending a substantial troop increase in order to conduct a counterinsurgency (COIN) campaign in Afghanistan.[52] Ultimately, the President's decision was to deploy an additional 30,000 American troops with a focus on building Afghanistan's security forces that the President described as "neither counterinsurgency nor nation building".[53] Even after receiving the specific language of the President's decision, Woodward writes that the military felt they had "outsmarted the President and had won" and that "counterinsurgency was alive and well."[54] Whether this was an example of a COIN group think mentality among the military leaders, an example of the military believing their COIN strategy was superior to civilian alternatives, or a combination of both is debatable. However, the fact that the President believed he was not receiving adequate military options to formulate his foreign policy highlights this as an area for concern.

The fact that a majority of the civilian population does not understand the military is another area worthy of concern; especially when those civilians are among the legislative and executive branches of Government. From a national security perspective, resourcing the military and the utility of military force are the two areas of greatest concern. How the downward trend of military veterans serving in Congress and the executive branch will affect policy or legislative votes is difficult to determine because legislators typically do not reference their status as veterans or non-veterans as having influenced their voting decisions. Typically, voting records are measured along a legislator's personal ideology and/or party affiliation. However, some indication of how veteran status affects policy may be gleaned from comparing outcomes of different Congresses throughout American history.

In their book, *Choosing Your Battles, American Civil-Military Relations and the Use of Force*, Peter D. Feaver and Christopher Gelpi conclude that the opinions of civilian elite veterans track more closely with the opinions of active duty military officers than they do of non-veterans in the civilian elite.[55] Furthermore, they find that civilian elites with no military experience have more interventionist tendencies in their support of using military force as opposed to the active military and civilian elite veterans who approach the use of military force for *realpolitik* reasons or "interstate issues that represent a substantial threat to national security such as control of territory, the maintenance of geostrategic access and position, and the defense of allies."[56] In essence, the civilian elite and the active military/civilian elite veterans "views converge somewhat when considering potential *realpolitik* uses of force but diverge more sharply when considering potential interventionist uses of force."[57]

Armed with this information, Feaver and Glepi conducted a study of the relations between the United States and other countries from 1816 to 1992. As part of the study, Feaver and Gelpi recorded the veteran status of the executive and legislative branches of government each time the United States initiated the use of military force against a target country. What their study found was that "as the percentage of veterans serving in the executive branch and the legislature increases, the probability that the United States will initiate militarized disputes declines by nearly 90 percent."[58] The report also found that "the higher the proportion of veterans in government, the greater the level of force the United States would use" if military action was initiated.[59] What this study suggests is that veteran legislators are significantly less likely to use military force for foreign policy than their non-veteran counterparts. However, when force is used by veteran legislators, they wield that force at a much greater level akin to the Powell doctrine.[60] Based on Fevor and Gelpi's conclusions on the historical initiation of force, the trend of diminishing veterans in the executive and legislative branches of the United States government suggests a greater likelihood of the United States using military force, though in lesser numbers, as a tool of future foreign policy.

One of the disadvantages for non-veteran Congressmen is that they lack an intuitive or "gut level" instinct when it comes to military matters. This lack of intuitive understanding can potentially result in both over and under compensation on a variety of military issues that affect national security. Because of their lack of military experience, some non-veteran Congressmen may be hesitant or even unwilling to challenge certain Pentagon or military leader assertions on issues such as budget needs, equipment needs, and force structure. An article by Mark Thompson in the November 2011 issue of *Time* magazine offers an interesting but insightful anecdote into this very issue:

> Representative Howard "Buck" McKeon, the California Republican who heads the House Armed Services Committee, never served in uniform – an unthinkable arrangement just a few decades ago. McKeon was stumped in September when asked in public if the military's "tooth to tail" ratio – the share of trigger pullers as part of the entire force – had budged from its historic 10% level. "What is tooth to tail?" the chairman responded. "Congress cuts the military slack because of their lack of experience, "UNC's Kohn [Richard Kohn – Military Historian] says, "They don't have a sense of the institutions and the culture, so they're less likely to exercise insightful or determined oversight".[61]

Conversely, non-veteran Congressmen could also be overly critical of the military, wanting to apply business/corporate model mandates on the military without fully appreciating the tremendous difference between running a business and operating in a military organization. Understanding the utility of military force to solve problems, understanding military organizations and how they function, and understanding veterans' issues are critical to maintaining an effective national defense. With the trend of declining veterans serving in Congress, it is of vital importance for the military to articulate and educate the Congress on military capabilities and the resources required to achieve these desired capabilities.

Perhaps the most disheartening of all the divergences in the military-civilian gap is the unequal burden of shared national sacrifice between the military and the civilian public. From a historical perspective, exposure of the American public to a nationally shared sacrificial burden from 9/11 and the wars in Iraq and Afghanistan is at the lowest level for a time of war in American history. For example, there has been no conscription, no war taxes levied, no war oriented conservation or rationing, and no war bonds sold to support the nation's wars in Iraq and Afghanistan. In his speech to a joint session of congress nine days after the 9/11 attacks, President George W. Bush stated that American's were expected to "live your lives and hug your children…uphold the values of America… support the victims of this tragedy" and asked for the American peoples "continued participation and confidence in the American economy."[62] Essentially, President Bush asked for nothing out of the ordinary from the American people and by no means asked for anything that could be construed as an enormous sacrifice. With the exception of increased security screening delays in public transportation, Americans have, by and large, gone about their lives in much the same manner as before 9/11 and the wars in Afghanistan and Iraq.

In their book *War and Taxes*, authors Steven A. Bank, Kirk J. Stark, and Joseph J. Thorndike provide a historical account of America's war-time fiscal policies for the major American wars since the American Revolution. Their findings are that "in every major conflict except the current one, the country has raised taxes to fund increased military expenditures."[63] To the contrary, American citizens have been the benefactor of tax cuts since 9/11 and the wars in Afghanistan and Iraq are being financed through deficit spending. Without drastic changes, the current wars in Afghanistan and Iraq may be the first in American history to be completely financed by a spending model that shifts the shared national sacrifice associated with paying for wars onto future generations of Americans. Simply put, compared to past American wartime generations, the current American public, in general, has sacrificed very little in regards to 9/11 and the wars in Iraq and Afghanistan. By contrast, the military, along with other government organizations actively fighting the war on terror, have taken the bulk of the nation's burden and sacrificed the most of any segment of the population since the 9/11 attacks. The military has borne repeated combat deployments, long stretches of time away from families, and paid the price for the wars in both life and limb.

The lack of national burden sharing between the military and civilian society does have some national security implications. At the beginning of World War I, Representative Edward Little advocated the raising of a war time tax by stating that in addition to conscripting the youth for war "that you would conscript the wealth as well…Let their dollars die for this country too."[64] This idea raised by Representative Little has been lost in the current political environment by the fact that Congress has refused to raise taxes to finance the wars in Iraq and Afghanistan. Ultimately, the funding of the wars since 9/11 may prove to be more politically than economically motivated. If a war tax had been levied on the American public after 9/11 it is more likely that Americans would pay more attention to the wars in Iraq and Afghanistan and demanded better accountability for how those conflicts were unfolding. Political leaders understand the dynamic of the American public; if the public is largely unaffected, they are less likely to question the motives and activities for military force over the long term. A more pessimistic view would be that the Bush administration refused to raise taxes to pay for the war in Iraq, not from a conservative economic ideology standpoint, but rather to avoid a widespread taxpayer backlash over United States involvement in a country with only nebulous ties to the 9/11 attacks.

The lack of public participation, or shared sacrifice through the financing the wars, sets a dangerous precedent with detrimental future consequences. By financing the war through deficit spending, the nation's financial health is put at increased risk and contributes to the decline of American standing in the world economy. Additionally, if the public is not part of future national wartime efforts, then public disinterest becomes tacit approval for policies involving military force that may or may not be in the best national interest. In regards to a shared national sacrifice, perhaps George Washington said it best when he stated "It may be laid down as a primary position, and the basis of our system, that every Citizen who enjoys the protection of a free Government, owes not only a proportion of his property, but even of his personal services to the defence [sic] of it."[65]

Recommendations

To some degree, there will always be a military-civilian gap. The military is limited in size and only a small portion of the population can serve at any give time. There are several actions that both the military and civilian leaders can take to reduce the widening gap. The best way to spread understanding of the military is for the military to meet and engage the public. The military is currently doing this to a limited degree with public speaking outreach programs at the United States Army War College and the Command and General Staff College. These public speaking programs should be drastically expanded to include junior officers at their respective company grade educational courses as well. Some of the best public speakers in the military are retired general officers who have been known to captivate audiences with their speaking skills. A program that arranged for some of the more dynamic retired senior officers to speak at high school assemblies around the country would be an ideal way to introduce America's youth to the rich military heritage of the United States. Additionally, retired senior flag officers should be considered for adjunct professor positions at some of the elite civilian institutions in order to provide a military view to the liberal arts curriculums. Leveraging the National Guard and the Reserve forces must also be a part of any campaign of public engagement. As true citizen soldiers, the Guard and Reserves play a crucial role in bridging the understanding between the military and the civilian worlds as they hold both perspectives. Hosting public events at Guard and Reserve centers that allow the public to learn about the military could also be beneficial. Perhaps the best way to increase the military's engagement is to unleash the creativity of military leaders at all levels through directive guidance from the Chairman of the Joint Chiefs of Staff and Service Chiefs. This does not need to be a heavy, requirement-laden document but rather something that encourages leaders at all levels to seek opportunities for public engagement at local leadership levels. Officers at all levels have shown great creativity in building trust and good will with civilians in Iraq and Afghanistan; why not unleash their creative abilities to engage the United States public? The military should also increase its fellowships, working with industry, and especially resident advanced degree programs at civilian colleges to the maximum extent possible.

There are also things that civilian leaders can do to help reduce the military civilian gap. One of the biggest things civilian legislators could do is to simply recognize the lack of understanding of the military and take steps to help the public become better acquainted with the military. Simple measures such as publicly encouraging young people to consider joining the military and encouraging schools to imbed military history into their core history curriculum could have surprising results. From a legislative perspective, a balanced budget amendment could bring about a more equitable sharing of the national sacrifice for the nation's wars. A balanced budget amendment would at least require a thorough discussion of how any potential conflict would be funded and likely result in some kind of sacrifice by either cuts to existing programs/services, tax increases, or both.

Conclusion

The current United States all volunteer military is the best military in the world. From the ashes of the Vietnam War, the military's senior leaders committed themselves to creating this world class volunteer force by embracing racial diversity, technology, education, realistic training, discipline, and demanding high standards of conduct characterized by moral values that reflect what Abraham Lincoln referred to as "the better angels of our nature."[66] In obtaining this highly educated, well trained and disciplined force, there has been a widening of the gap between the military and civilian society. The military is increasingly seeing itself as being superior to society while society is increasingly becoming a stranger to the military's hardships and sacrifices. The fact that the military and civilian societies are becoming estranged is disconcerting but is far from the point of endangering the Republic. The United States military has always openly embraced the primacy of civilian authority; it's in the military's DNA regardless of how far apart civil-military relations may grow. However, military effectiveness, readiness, and even foreign policy can benefit from a narrowing of the military-civilian gap. Both the military and civilian leadership have a responsibility to find mutual understanding and to work cooperatively to lesson the military-civilian gap. Perhaps Sir William F. Butler best described the detriment of a military-civilian gap in 1889 when he stated "The nation that will insist upon drawing a broad line of demarcation between the fighting man and the thinking man is liable to find its fighting done by fools and its thinking by cowards."[67]

Endnotes

[1] U.S. Constitution, Preamble.

[2] The total WWII US service members was divided by the total US population of 1946 to arrive at the 11.4% ratio. Sources for the calculations are the VA America's Wars fact sheet (http://www.va.gov/opa/publications/factsheets/fs_americas_wars.pdf) November 2011, and the US Census Bureau's Historical National Population Estimates: July 1, 1900 to July 1, 1999 (http://www.census.gov/popest/data/national/totals/pre-1980/tables/popclockest.txt), April 2011.

[3] Mary Margaret Sudduth, *Annual Demographic Profile of the Department of Defense Active Duty and U.S. Coast Guard Forces Profile FY 2010* (Patrick AFB, FL: Defense Equal Opportunity Management Institute, 2010), 9.

[4] Karen R. Humes, Nicholas A. Jones, Roberto R. Ramirez, *Overview of Race and Hispanic Origin: 2010* (Washington, DC: United States Census Bureau, March 2011), 4.

[5] Multiple Government agencies provide yearly demographic data of which were examined for basic trends. Unfortunately, no two data sources matched in total numbers of service members for any given year, however all data sources tended to point out the same trends and were relatively close in their overall percentages of racial representation in the United States military. Yearly racial data from the Defense Equal Opportunity Institute from 1999 to 2010 (http://www.deomi.org/EOEEOResources/DemographicReports.cfm), the Deputy Under Secretary of Defense for Military Community and Family Policy (Demographic Profile of the Military Community for fiscal years 2003 to 2010, http://www.militaryhomefront.dod.mil./pls/psgprod/f?p=MHF:DETAIL0:0::::CID:20.20.60.70.0.0.0.0.0), the Office of the Under Secretary of Defense for Personnel and Readiness (Population and Representation in the Military Services, http://prhome.defense.gov/MPP/ACCESSION%20POLICY/poprep.aspx), and data from the United States Census Bureau were used for comparison.

[6] Harry S. Truman, "Executive Order 9981," July 26, 1948, linked from the *Truman Library Home Page* at "Research, Executive Orders," http://www.trumanlibrary.org/9981a.htm (accessed February 8, 2012).

[7] Charles C. Moskos, John Sibley Butler, *All That We Can Be: Black Leadership and Racial Integration the Army Way* (New York, NY: BasicBooks, 1996) 1, 2.

[8] John R. Logan, Wenquan Zhang, *Global Neighborhoods: New Evidence from Census 2010* (Providence, RI: US2010 Project, November 11), 1.

⁹ Office of the Undersecretary of Defense for Personnel and Readiness, *Population and Representation in the Military Services FY2010* (Washington, DC: U.S. Department of Defense, 2010), Appendix D (Historical Data), Table D-10, 13. Appendix B (Active Component Enlisted Accessions, Enlisted Force, Officer Accessions, and Officer Corps Tables), Table B-46 contains the specific states that comprise the different geographic regions of Northeast, North Central, South, and West which match the US Census Bureau's definitions of these regions.

¹⁰ Ibid.

¹¹ U.S. Census Bureau, "Annual Estimates of the Population for the United States, Regions, States, and Puerto Rico: April 1, 2010 to July 1, 2011," http://www.census.gov/popest/data/state/totals/2011/tables/NST-EST2011-02.xls (accessed February 12, 2012).

¹² Office of the Undersecretary of Defense for Personnel and Readiness, *Population and Representation in the Military Services FY2010*, Appendix B (Active Component Enlisted Accessions, Enlisted Force, Officer Accessions, and Officer Corps Tables), Table B-48, 92-100.

¹³ Ibid., 96.

¹⁴ Ibid., 93.

¹⁵ A comparison of data from the 1996 to 2009 Defense, Personnel and Readiness, Population and Representation data provides similar numbers to those presented in the FY 2010 report. The data can be found for each fiscal year in Appendix B of the particular fiscal year report. The FY1996 to FY2002 data can be found in Table B-1, the FY2003 to FY2006 data can be found in Table B-11, the FY2007 to FY 2008 data can be found in Table B-4, and FY2009 data can be found in Table B-48. All reports are accessible from the following website: http://prhome.defense.gov/MPP/ACCESSION%20POLICY/poprep.aspx.

¹⁶ Secretary of Defense for Military Community and Family Policy, *Demographics 2010, Profile of the Military Community* (Washington DC: U.S. Department of Defense, 2010), 27.

¹⁷ Ivy League Presidential ticket candidates since 1932 are as follows:

Election Year	Candidate	Ivy League School	Election Year	Candidate	Ivy League School
1932	Franklin D. Roosevelt	Harvard/Columbia	1984	George H.W. Bush	Yale
1936	Franklin D. Roosevelt	Harvard/Columbia	1988	George H.W. Bush	Yale
1940	Franklin D. Roosevelt	Harvard/Columbia		Michael Dukakis	Harvard
1944	Franklin D. Roosevelt	Harvard/Columbia	1992	George H.W. Bush	Yale
	Thomas E. Dewey	Columbia		William J. Clinton	Yale
1948	Thomas E. Dewey	Columbia		Albert A. Gore Jr.	Harvard
1952	Adlai Stevenson	Princeton	1996	William J. Clinton	Yale
1956	Adlai Stevenson	Princeton		Albert A. Gore Jr.	Harvard
1960	John F. Kennnedy	Harvard	2000	George W. Bush	Yale
	Henry C. Lodge Jr.	Harvard		Albert A. Gore Jr.	Harvard
1968	Edmund Muskie	Cornell		Joseph Lieberman	Yale
1972	Sargent Shriver	Yale	2004	George W. Bush	Yale
1976	Gerald Ford	Yale		John Kerry	Yale
1980	George H.W. Bush	Yale	2008	Barrack H. Obama	Harvard

[18] US News and World Report, "The Top 10 Colleges for Members of Congress", Michael Morella, accessed 7 January 2011, http://www.usnews.com/news/slideshows/the-top-10-colleges-for-members-of-congress

[19] US News and World Report, "Where the Fortune 500 CEOs Went to College", Brian Burnsed, 3 January 2011, http://www.usnews.com/education/articles/2011/01/03/where-the-fortune-500-ceos-went-to-college (accessed January 15, 2012).

[20] Frank Schaeffer, Kathy Roth-Douquet, *AWOL, The Unexcused Absence of America's Upper Classes from Military Service* (New York, NY: Harper Collins, 2006), 43.

[21] Eliot A. Cohen, "ROTC's Hard Road Back To Campus," *The Washington Post*, December 22, 2010.

[22] Jennifer E. Manning, *Membership of the 112th Congress: A Profile* (Washington, DC: U.S. Library of Congress, Congressional Research Service, March 1, 2011), 8.

[23] Ibid.

[24] Mildred L. Amer, *Membership of the 107th Congress: A Profile* (Washington, DC: U.S. Library of Congress, Congressional Research Service, December 19, 2001), 5.

[25] Manning, *Membership of the 112th Congress: A Profile*, 7.

[26] William T. Bianco, Jamie Markham, "Vanishing Veterans: The Decline of Military Experience in the U.S. Congress" in *Soldiers and Civilians, The Civil-Military Gap and American National Security*, ed. Peter D. Feaver and Richard H. Kohn (Cambridge, MA: MIT Press, 2001), 283.

[27] At the time of this paper, only one of the four Republican candidates seeking the Republican nomination for President have military experience. The only veteran candidate is Ron Paul (USAF veteran). The current Republican front runner, Mitt Romney and the remaining two candidates, Newt Gingrich, and Rick Santorum, have no direct military experience.

[28] Bianco, Markham "Vanishing Veterans", 282.

[29] "Army Brats" may be the exception to this rule, where many grow up in households that operate on military time, and endure countless other peculiarities insisted upon by one or both parents who happen to be or once were serving members of the Armed Forces.

[30] Eliot A. Cohen, "Civil – Military Relations" in *America the Vulnerable, Our Military Problems and How To Fix Them*, ed. John F. Lehman and Harvey Sicherman (Philadelphia, PA: Foreign Policy Research Institute, 2001), 88.

[31] Charles Moskos, "Values and Ethics", *All Things Considered*, National Public Radio, September 11, 1997.

[32] For examples of these types of recruiting materials see U.S. Air Force Recruiting commercial "Cyber Defense" at http://www.youtube.com/watch?v=t849CYRd2Ak, "It's not Science Fiction" at http://www.youtube.com/watch?v=bg9K1mCh65U&feature=related, and the

U.S. Navy commercial "Called to Serve" at http://www.youtube.com/watch?v=F1G3QW31J9o&feature=related.

[33] The United States Marine Corps has commonly used the slogan, "The few, the proud, the Marines" while evoking images of an elite fighting force. Examples of this imagery can be found at http://www.youtube.com/watch?v=mR_2tLsJuf0&feature=related and http://www.youtube.com/watch?v=qwmBu3LK6Ik&feature=relmfu.

[34] Barbara A. Bicksler, Lisa G. Nolan, *Recruiting an All Volunteer Force: The Need for Sustained Investment in Recruiting Resources, An Update* (Arlington, VA: Strategic Analysis Inc, December 2009) 6, 7.

[35] Secretary of Defense for Military Community and Family Policy, *Demographics 2010, Profile of the Military Community*, 33

[36] U.S. Censes Bureau, "Educational Attainment of the Population 18 Years and Over, by Age, Sex, Race, and Hispanic Origin: 2010," http://www.census.gov/hhes/socdemo/education/data/cps/2010/Table1-01.xls (accessed January 15, 2012).

[37] Office of the Undersecretary of Defense for Personnel and Readiness, *Population and Representation in the Military Services FY2010*, Appendix D (Historical Data) Table D-9, 12. For AFQT scores, the reference group is a sample of 18 to 23 year old youth who took the ASVAB as part of a national norming study conducted in 1997. Thus, an AFQT score of 90 indicates that the examinee scored as well as or better than 90% of the nationally-representative sample of 18 to 23 year old youth. An AFQT score of 50 indicates that the examinee scored as well as or better than 50% of the nationally-representative sample.

[38] Ibid.

[39] Cohen, "Civil – Military Relations," 89.

[40] Pew Research Center also uses the term "public" or "general public" to refer to the civilian population in the study.

[41] Pew Research Center, *The Military-Civilian Gap, War and Sacrifice in the Post 9/11 Era*, (Washington, DC: Pew Social & Demographic Trends, October 5, 2011), 3.

[42] Ibid.

[43] Heidi A. Urben, "Civil-Military Relations in a Time of War: Party, Politics, and the Profession of Arms" PhD diss., Georgetown University, April 14, 2010, Table B-2, 39.

[44] Ole R. Holsti, "Of Chasms and Convergences: Attitudes and Beliefs of Civilians and Military Elites at the Start of a New Millennium" in *Soldiers and Civilians, The Civil-Military Gap and American National Security*, ed. Peter D. Feaver and Richard H. Kohn (Cambridge, MA: MIT Press, 2001) 28. The TISS survey showed that veterans identified themselves as 36.9% Republican, 31% Democrat, and 27.6% Independent whereas the non-veterans identified themselves as 29.1% Republican, 33% Democrat, and 32.9% Independent. The survey also found that military officers identified themselves as 63.9% Republican, 8.1% Democrat, and 16.7% Independent.

[45] Pew Research Center, *The Military-Civilian Gap, War and Sacrifice in the Post 9/11 Era*, 65.

[46] Ibid., 64.

[47] Ibid., 38.

[48] Ibid., 63, 64.

[49] Ibid., 59.

[50] Ibid.

[51] Bob Woodward, *Obama's Wars* (New York, NY: Simon & Schuster, 2010), 157 – 333.

[52] Ibid., 257, 258, 311.

[53] Ibid., 325.

[54] Ibid., 332.

[55] Peter D. Feaver, Christopher Gelpi, *Choosing Your Battles, American Civil-Military Relations and the Use of Force* (Princeton, NJ: Princeton University Press, 2004) 6.

[56] Ibid., 5, 6.

[57] Ibid., 6.

[58] Ibid., 7.

[59] Ibid.

[60] The "Powell doctrine" is a phrase coined to reflect General Colin Powell's guidelines for the use of force one of which is that if force is to be used it should be decisive or overwhelming force.

[61] Mark Thompson, "The Other 1%", *Time*, November 21, 2011, 38, 39.

[62] George W. Bush, "Text of President Bush's Address to a Joint Session of Congress and the Nation", September 20, 2001, linked from *The Washington Post Home Page* at http://www.washingtonpost.com/wp-srv/nation/specials/attacked/transcripts/bushaddress092001.html (accessed January 16, 2012).

[63] Steven A. Bank, Kirk J. Stark, Joseph J. Thorndike, *War and Taxes* (Washington, DC: The Urban Institute Press, 2008), 167.

[64] Ibid., 173.

[65] George Washington, "Sentiments On a Peace Establishment" in *The Writings of George Washington from the Original Manuscript Sources 1745-1799 Volume 26*, ed. John C. Fitzpatrick (Washington, DC: Government Printing Office, July 1938), 389.

[66] Abraham Lincoln, "First Inaugural Address", March 4, 1861, linked from the *Bartleby.com Home Page* at http://www.bartleby.com/124/pres31.html (accessed January 18, 2012)

[67] Sir William F. Butler, *English Men of Action, Charles George Gordon* (London: Macmillan and Co., 1889), 85.